EDGE BOOKS™

Investigating Unsolved Mysteries

# ALIENS AND UFOS

## MYTH OR REALITY?

by Lori Hile

CAPSTONE PRESS
a capstone imprint

Edge Books are published by Capstone Press,
1710 Roe Crest Drive, North Mankato, Minnesota 56003
www.mycapstone.com

**Library of Congress Cataloging-in-Publication Data**
Names: Hile, Lori, author.
Title: Aliens and UFOs  : myth or reality? / by Lori Hile.
Description: Capstone Press : North Mankato, Minnesota, [2019] | Series: Edge
    books. Investigating unsolved mysteries. | Includes bibliographical references and
index. | Audience: Ages 8-14.
Identifiers: LCCN 2018010989 (print) | LCCN 2018013662 (ebook) |
    ISBN 9781543535785 (eBook PDF) |
    ISBN 9781543535709 (hardcover) |
    ISBN 9781543535747 (pbk.)
Subjects: LCSH: Unidentified flying objects—Sightings and encounters—Juvenile
    literature. | Extraterrestrial beings—Juvenile literature.
Classification: LCC TL789.2 (ebook) | LCC TL789.2 .H55 2019 (print) | DDC 001.942—
    c23
LC record available at https://lccn.loc.gov/2018010989

**Editorial Credits**
Abby Colich, editor; Kayla Rossow, designer; Morgan Walters, photo researcher;
Gene Bentdahl, production specialist

**Photo Credits**
Alamy: Chronicle, top right 7, geogphotos, bottom right 9; Getty Images: Universal
History Archive, top right 13; Shutterstock: adike, bottom right 28, Aphelleon, 4, BJ
Ray, background 21, drewthehobbit, background 13, Edward Haylan, top right 19,
Elesey, (light) Cover, Everett Historical, top middle 21, Faina Gurevich, bottom 27, Fer
Gregory, top 29, top 30, FWStudio, (chalk texture) design element throughout, Igor
Zh, (background) Cover, bottom right 5, lassedesignen, 1, M. Cornelius, spread 2-3,
14, background 23, Maksimilian, background 25, background 32, back cover, Michael
Dorogovich, middle 17, mRGB, background 17, nexus 7, background 11, NikoNomad,
background 27, Pavel Chagochkin, middle 31, Smileus, background 9, SONTAYA
CHAISAMUTR, background 19, Strelyuk, top right 11, Styve Reineck, bottom middle
25, Tobin Akehurst, background 7, Tom Tom, background 5, u3d, (ufo) Cover, Ursatii,
middle right 23, Vadim Sadovski, background 15, background 28

Printed and bound in the USA.    PA017

# TABLE OF CONTENTS

# Introduction

# UP IN THE AIR

Have you ever looked up at the sky and seen something you didn't recognize? You might have witnessed a UFO, or Unidentified Flying Object. Some people think these objects are from other planets. Many say they have seen creatures on board UFOs. These creatures are called **extraterrestrials** or aliens. Sometimes they even look like humans.

What could these UFOs really be? Where do they come from? Do they truly exist? What do you think? Read a few stories about people who claim to have seen UFOs and aliens. Can science solve the mystery?

extraterrestrial—a life-form that comes from outer space

# Close Encounters

In 1971 a UFO investigator named Alan Hynek grouped UFO sightings into three areas. A fourth was added later.

- **Close encounters of the first kind:**
  A witness sees an object or lights in the sky that cannot be identified.
- **Close encounters of the second kind:**
  A UFO has a physical effect on the things around it. It may cause injuries, frighten animals, or stall a car's engine.
- **Close encounters of the third kind:**
  A witness sees an alien creature.
- **Close encounters of the fourth kind:**
  A witness interacts with an alien.

# CHAPTER 1
# CLOSE ENCOUNTERS AND ALIEN ABDUCTIONS

It was a cloudless day in June 1947. Pilot Kenneth Arnold flew over Washington's Cascade Mountains. Arnold was searching for an airplane that had crashed. Suddenly, a blinding flash of light interrupted his search. Arnold looked out of the window. All he could see was a distant airplane.

Soon, more flashes caught his eye. He saw nine odd-looking objects. The wingless metallic objects moved quickly. Arnold tried to measure their speed. He guessed they were moving at 1,700 miles (2,735 kilometers) per hour. That's twice the speed of sound! No plane in 1947 could fly that fast. Had Arnold seen alien spacecraft?

Kenneth Arnold stands next to the aircraft he was flying the day he saw the unidentified flashes.

## FACT

UFOs are sometimes called flying saucers. Arnold was the first to describe them this way. His sighting was also one of the first official UFO reports.

## A Glowing Pyramid

On December 26, 1980, something crashed near an air force base in England. Shortly after midnight, security officer James Penniston came to investigate. Penniston and two airmen arrived at the crash site. They saw a glowing object. It was so bright Penniston had to squint.

The object was about 9 feet (2.7 meters) long and 6.5 feet (2 m) tall. It was shaped like a pyramid. Blue and yellow lights swirled around it. The air felt electrically charged. The men's radios crackled. Penniston touched the craft's surface. Tiny symbols were carved on it. It looked metallic, yet it felt warm and smooth, like fabric.

Penniston took notes for about an hour. Then the object grew brighter and lifted off the ground. Once it cleared the trees, it shot off quickly. Penniston wrote in his notebook, "Speed: Impossible!"

 This statue now sits near the spot where the UFOs landed.

9

## Bizarre Black Dust

One night in January 1988, Sean Knowles was driving with his family and two dogs. They were on a lonely stretch of road in Australia. Suddenly, the radio failed. Knowles spotted a strange ball of light floating in front of their car. The object was shaped like a giant egg in a cup. It was just under 3 feet (1 m) wide.

The object landed on top of the car. Then it sucked the car off the road! Sean's mother, Faye, stretched her arm out the window. She touched the object. It felt warm and spongy. Then she pulled her hand back in. It was caked in a strange black dust. The dogs started barking.

Suddenly, the object slammed the car back onto the road. The family drove to the nearest gas station. Faye's hand swelled. The dogs lost clumps of hair. Had Faye touched an alien or UFO?

## FACT
The Knowles family reported the scary story to the gas station worker. The worker told them a truck driver had seen a similar ball of light.

# Betty and Barney Hill

In September 1961 Barney and Betty Hill were driving through the mountains of New Hampshire. A bright light kept pace with their car. At first they thought it might be a **satellite** or an airplane. Soon Betty spotted colored lights and a circular row of windows. Barney pulled over. He saw small figures in dark uniforms peering out of the windows!

The Hills took off in their car. Soon they heard an odd beeping sound. They felt a tingling sensation. Before they knew it, two hours had passed. They were 35 miles (56 km) farther down the road. At home, they discovered their watches had stopped working. Betty had nightmares that she'd been taken aboard an alien spacecraft. Barney developed a rash and an **ulcer**.

The Hills underwent **hypnosis**. They recalled short creatures with large, bald heads and dark, almond-shaped eyes. The creatures had taken them on board the craft. They took samples of their skin, saliva, blood, hair, and nails.

Betty and Barney Hill with a newspaper article about their experience ▼

# Memory Test

Professor Alvin H. Lawson put a random group of people under hypnosis. He asked them to imagine being abducted by aliens. Their stories were very similar to those of abductees—with one big difference. The real abductees experienced fear and sadness while remembering their stories. Lawson thought this made it clear that the abductees had actually experienced some sort of trauma.

# CHAPTER 2

# USING SCIENCE TO INVESTIGATE

Throughout the ages, people have reported strange visions in the skies. Even ancient Egyptians reported unexplained objects in the sky.

Are witnesses imagining things? Are they exaggerating their stories? Are some of them lying? Many people believe that UFOs are alien spacecraft. Others believe that UFOs have more "down to earth" explanations.

# The Scientific Method

Can the mystery of UFOs and aliens ever be solved? Look at the evidence in the stories. Can it be tested with the scientific method? Good investigators follow the scientific method. They use the method to establish a **theory** and test a **hypothesis**. The scientific method has a few basic steps:

- Ask questions.
- Do background research.
- Put together an idea, called a hypothesis.
- Test your hypothesis with an experiment.
- Study the results of your experiment. What did you learn?
- Draw conclusions. Based on your results, is your idea true? Is it partially true? Or is it completely untrue?
- Tell people about your results.

**theory**—an idea that brings together several hypotheses to explain something

**hypothesis**—a prediction that can be tested

## UFO or IFO?

Most people who report UFOs are not seeing UFOs at all. Records show that 75 to 90 percent of UFO sightings are ordinary objects. This makes them IFOs (Identified Flying Objects), not UFOs. So what are these IFOs?

## Flying Pelicans

Remember the nine metallic objects that pilot Kenneth Arnold saw? One researcher believes that those "flying saucers" were actually pelicans! The birds can fly at very high **altitudes**. The sun reflects off their oily feathers. The light makes them glisten like metal. Pelicans also fly high and fast. Their wingspan can reach almost 9 feet (2.7 m).

## The Venus Trap

In April 1966 two American police officers chased a bright, disc-shaped object through two states. Investigators concluded that the men had been chasing Venus. This bright planet was rising at the time. Reports of UFO sightings increase whenever Venus is especially bright in the sky.

**altitude**—how high a place is above sea level or Earth's surface

**lenticular**—having the shape of a lens, where both sides curve outward

## Human-Made Objects

Some human-made objects are also mistaken for UFOs. Every day more than 800 weather balloons float in the sky. These teardrop-shaped balloons send information about the weather back to Earth. They are often mistaken for UFOs. Weather balloons can be as wide as a bus. When they reflect sunlight, they can cast an eerie glow.

Most airplanes are easy to recognize. But many people are fooled by less common flying machines. Helicopters, airplanes towing banners, and fighter planes can look like UFOs. Blimps or satellites may also look like UFOs to some. People may see one of these objects from an odd angle and not recognize it. Or they may not be familiar with the object in the first place.

Experimental military aircraft fool even more people. These aircraft are sometimes shaped like triangles or even saucers. The aircraft may be top secret. The military often denies their existence. This leads witnesses to believe they are UFOs.

A weather balloon floats through the sky.

# Hoaxes

About 5 percent of UFO sightings turn out to be hoaxes. One of the most famous fakes came in 1996. Movie producer Ray Santilli released shocking footage. It showed doctors removing organs from the body of a dead alien. In 2006 Santilli admitted that he had created most of the footage himself.

# CHAPTER 3

# EVIDENCE AND THEORIES

 Proven hoaxes and cases of mistaken identity account for most UFO reports. But up to one-fifth of sightings remain unexplained. Are these truly alien spacecraft? Study the evidence and theories. Then decide what you think.

## Mariana Mystery

In August 1950 Nick Mariana owned a baseball team in Great Falls, Montana. One day before a game he wanted to check the weather. So he climbed to the top of his stadium. Mariana noticed two bright, silvery discs, spinning slowly overhead. He grabbed a camera and filmed the objects.

The U.S. Air Force said that the objects were shadows of fighter jets. But Mariana says that he saw fighter jets after the discs disappeared. Many others have studied the film. Most believe it is genuine. It was difficult to fake films at the time. Most agree that the objects are not fighter jets. But it is impossible to prove exactly what they were.

Did Nick Mariana really see UFOs?
Or were they fighter jets similar to these?

## FACT
Investigators looked at Mariana's video
again in 1952, 1956, and 1966. They were
never able to confirm if the objects
were aircraft or something else.

## The Belgian Triangle Photo

Between November 1989 and April 1990, something strange happened in Belgium. Flat, triangle-shaped objects with twinkling lights lit up the skies. Thousands of people saw them. Only one clear photo surfaced. A young man called Patrick M. snapped it. NASA scientists and other researchers looked at the photo. Most believed it was genuine. But in July 2011, Patrick M. admitted that he had faked the photo.

The fake photo does not disprove that the Belgian triangles were UFOs. But it does show why photos alone cannot prove anything about what people see in the sky. Photos are easy to fake using models or computers. Fake photos can be difficult to detect.

## Radar

On July 19, 1952, people watched orange, glowing objects zigzag over Washington, D.C. **Radar** at two nearby airports also observed several unknown objects flying at high speeds. Radar has supported 74 other UFO sightings. These include the Belgian triangles. Radar errors are possible but highly unlikely.

This photo may look like a real UFO, but it is a fake.

## Landing Traces

Photos may not be the best way to learn about UFOs. But what if UFOs left something behind? Sometimes they do! Investigators call these traces. UFOs have left behind more than 5,000 traces. Traces include burn marks, imprints, rings, and **radiation**. For example, investigators at the air force base in England found three 7-inch (18-centimeter) indentations at the landing site. Radiation levels at the site were eight times higher than normal.

## Medical Effects

After her UFO encounter, Faye Knowles became sick. Researchers studied the black dust left on her car. They found traces of a radioactive chemical. The chemical can cause sickness. Some 400 other UFO sightings also include reports of illnesses or injuries. Although they are interesting, it is difficult to prove anything from the medical effects of UFO contact.

## Wormhole Theory

A wormhole is a possible shortcut through space and time. If wormholes exist, they could more quickly bridge the space between two distant places. Aliens could travel to Earth through wormholes. This theory may explain why some UFOs seem to appear out of nowhere.

## Another Dimension

Most people easily recognize three dimensions. They are up-down, left-right, and across. But scientists believe that up to 11 other dimensions exist. Some researchers suggest that aliens may exist in another dimension. Aliens may "cross over" into a dimension where we can see them.

# CHAPTER 4

# CAN THE MYSTERY BE SOLVED?

Not all UFO sightings are the same. Some people may have seen clouds. Others may have seen weather balloons or military aircraft. But a small number of UFO sightings appear to be objects that we cannot identify.

So far, no one has found hard, physical evidence that proves UFOs are from outer space. Until such evidence is available, it cannot be proven that UFOs are anything other than earthly objects.

## Signs of Openness

Government agencies in France, the United Kingdom, and the United States recently released UFO records to the public. The records show that most governments have taken UFO reports seriously. Scientists must have access to complete UFO data. They must also be encouraged to investigate. Only then can the mystery of UFOs and aliens ever be solved.

## Chances of Life

Scientists estimate that there are 300 sextillion stars in the universe. That means life could exist in many different places. Some scientists believe life likely exists on other planets. However, this idea has yet to be proven.

 A woman in Colorado built this watchtower. She wanted to encourage others to look for UFOs.

# SUMMING UP THE SCIENCE

Now that you've read about aliens and UFOs, what do you think? Can you use the scientific method to prove UFOs and life outside of Earth exists or not?

In some cases, it's easy to use the scientific method. Sometimes scientists can test a photo to show that it was faked. Or the military can prove one of its planes was flying at the time and place someone thought they saw a UFO.

Other times, it's more difficult. People witness things in the sky that have no explanation. We can use the scientific method to prove these sightings were not something else. But until an alien or UFO stays behind on Earth, we can't prove that life from outer space exists.

So what is the answer? It's very possible that there is life on other planets. But until we have evidence that proves it, we can't know for sure. That doesn't mean you can't have fun making up your own ideas about the life that may exist in outer space.

 Do you think life-forms from space look like this?

# TIMELINE

**11,000 BCE**   An ancient Egyptian scroll describes people watching circles of fire in the sky. They throw themselves to the ground in fear.

**200 to 600 BCE**   Animal and geometric patterns are carved in the Nazca Desert in southern Peru. These patterns can only be seen from high above.

**1300s CE**   A painting of the crucifixion shows a man traveling through the sky in an egg-shaped vehicle.

**1947**   Pilot Kenneth Arnold sees nine metallic objects skipping through the sky. His is one of the first official UFO reports of modern times.

**1947**   An object crashes on a farmer's field near Roswell, New Mexico. The U.S. government first says it was a flying saucer, then a weather balloon, and then a top-secret type of balloon.

**1950**   Baseball team owner Nick Mariana films two UFOs floating over his stadium.

**1961**   Betty and Barney Hill experience what they describe as an abduction into a spacecraft. They claim they were given medical exams.

**1980**   A mysterious pyramid-shaped object lands in Rendlesham Forest, near Bentwaters Air Force Base in England.

**1989 to 1990**   Thousands of residents witness bright, flat, triangular objects in the skies over Belgium.

**1996**   Movie producer Ray Santilli releases footage of a dead alien he says he filmed in 1947, after the Roswell crash.

**2006**   Ray Santilli admits his alien autopsy footage was fake.

**2012**   A newspaper in Jordan publishes a story about an alien invasion. The story leads to panic before readers learn it was an April Fools' Day joke.

**2017**   A former Pentagon employee says he ran a government program from 2007 to 2012 that investigated possible UFOs.

# GLOSSARY

**altitude** (AL-ti-tood)—how high a place is above sea level or Earth's surface

**extraterrestrial** (ek-struh-tuh-RESS-tree-uhl)—a life-form that comes from outer space

**hypnosis** (hip-NOH-siss)—the process of putting someone in a trancelike state; sometimes used to bring back memories

**hypothesis** (hye-POTH-uh-siss)—a prediction that can be tested about how a scientific investigation or experiment will turn out

**lenticular** (len-TICK-yoo-luhr)—having the shape of a lens, where both sides curve outward

**radar** (RAY-dar)—a device that uses radio waves to track the location of objects

**radiation** (ray-dee-AY-shuhn)—tiny particles sent out from radioactive material

**satellite** (SAT-uh-lite)—a spacecraft used to send signals and information from one place to another

**theory** (THEER-ee)—an idea that brings together several hypotheses to explain something

**ulcer** (UHL-sehr)—a sore inside the body, usually in the stomach

# READ MORE

**Kenney, Karen Latchana**. *Mysterious UFOs and Aliens.* Fear Fest. Minneapolis: Lerner Publications, 2017.

**Loh-Hagan, Virginia**. *Roswell.* Don't Read Alone! Ann Arbor, Mich.: Cherry Lake Publishing, 2017.

**McCollum, Sean**. *Handbook of UFOs, Crop Circles, and Alien Encounters.* Paranormal Handbooks. North Mankato, Minn.: Capstone Press, 2017.

# INTERNET SITES

Use FactHound to find Internet sites related to this book.

Visit *www.facthound.com*

Just type in 9781543535709 and go.

# INDEX